Read on to find all the instructions you will need to complete our cross stitch and needlepoint designs.

titch across it. If you are working over one thread such as with 14HPI aida then you will have to split the threads in the centre. Where two different symbols share a square on the chart, one is a three-quarter stitch in one colour and one is a quarter stitch in another colour. It is up to you which colour you choose to be which but it is best if the three quarter stitch is in the colour you want to be more prominent.

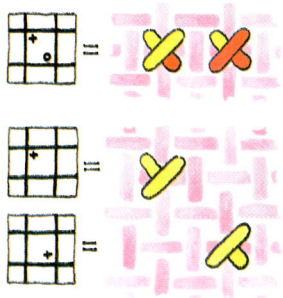

How to Stitch Backstitch

The solid and dotted lines on the charts represent backstitch. Follow these lines using the number of strands indicated in each key. Bring the needle up one square to the right of where the line begins, then push it in at the beginning of the line. Bring the needle up to the right of the first stitch and continue always working back on yourself.

How to Stitch French Knots

Bring the needle up where you want the knot to be. Hold the thread where it comes out of the fabric with your left hand. For a small knot twist the needle around the thread once; for a large knot, twist it round two or three times. Holding the thread taut, push the needle down into the fabric close to where it emerged.

When the needle is half way through the fabric, tighten the thread close up to the needle to form a knot. Continue pushing the needle and thread back to the wrong side of the fabric.

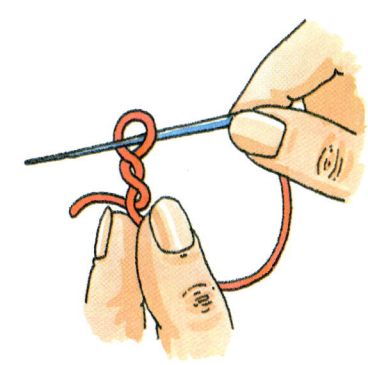

How to Work Continental Tent Stitch

Continental Tent stitch is worked in rows from left to right and then from right to left, with a long slanted stitch on the back. If you are working from the left come up at the top of the stitch and down at the bottom and, when returning from the right, come up at the bottom and down at the top. You will be coming up into holes which have already been stitched, so care must be taken not to disturb the existing threads in the holes.

How to Stitch over Two Threads

If you are working on a high count fabric such as 28HPI evenweave or linen, it is usual to stitch over two threads of the fabric. This will give the same finished design area as 14HPI aida. (Likewise, if you are working on 36HPI linen you will get the same area as 18HPI aida.) Make each cross over two threads to cover a nine hole square instead of the usual four hole square.

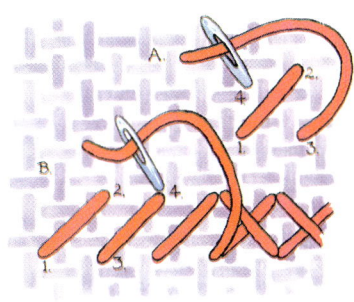

How to Wash your Finished Stitching

If you notice any marks on your finished work, you can wash it.

1 Immerse the stitched piece in luke-warm water. If the colours start to run, don't worry, just keep rinsing until the water runs clear. If there are any stubborn stains, rub a little detergent on to the area until the stain is removed.

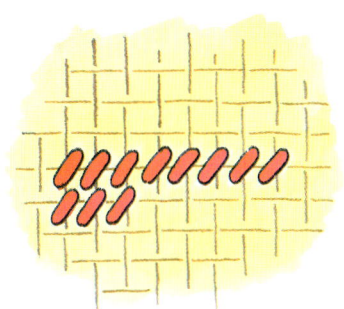

thick, clean, white towel. Place your work right side down on this with a thin clean cloth over it. Press carefully until the fabric is dry. The thickness of the towel will prevent you from flattening the stitches.

4 Iron into the stitches with the point of the iron in a circular motion - this will raise the stitches and improve their appearance. Avoid having the iron too hot or pressing too hard.

How to Block your Needlepoint Canvas

You Will Need:
- Flat clean board
- Blotting paper
- Drawing pins

1 If the canvas has very little distortion, it will only need to be steam pressed to even out the stitch surface.

2 If, your canvas is not square, then dampen it lightly or spray with water to soften the canvas.

3 Mark the finished size of the canvas on to the blotting paper and place the canvas face down on it. Pull the canvas square to match up with the lines on the paper.

4 Pin the canvas, outside the stitching area, on to the board. Only remove the canvas when it is totally dry – this process can take several days.

How to Lace your Work for Framing

1 Cut a piece of acid free mount board to the same size as the inside of the frame. This will be your lacing board.

2 If you want to use a coloured mount inside your frame then cut a piece of 2oz wadding to the same size as the mount opening. If you are not using a mount then cut the wadding to the size of the frame opening. Place the wadding centrally on the lacing board.

3 Centre your stitched fabric right side up over the wadding and lacing board. Push pins through the fabric and into the board along the top edge. Use the holes of the fabric as a guide to ensure that you pin it straight.

4 Pull the fabric gently and pin along the bottom in the same way. Repeat this for the other two sides.

5 Working form the back of the board, thread a large-eyed needle with thick strong cotton such as crochet cotton and tie a knot at the end. Lace form top bottom using an under and over motion. Stop half way across the back and repeat the lacing for the other side. When you reach the centre, go back and remove the slack form the threads by pulling them tightly one by one. Tie the two ends in a knot at the centre.

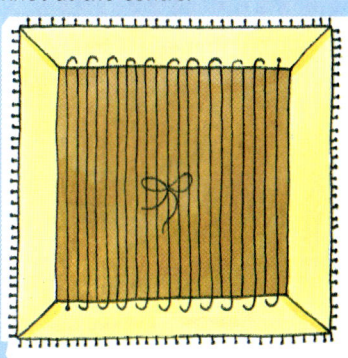

6 Repeat this process from side to side. If at any stage you run out of thread before you reach the centre, join a new piece with a reef knot.

7 Fold in the corners and stitch into place then remove the pins. Your work is now ready to be framed in the frame of your choice.

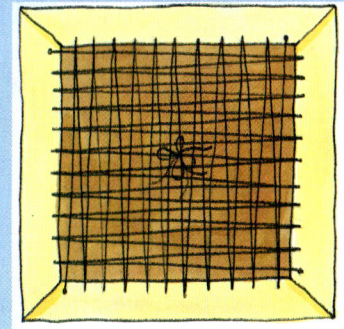

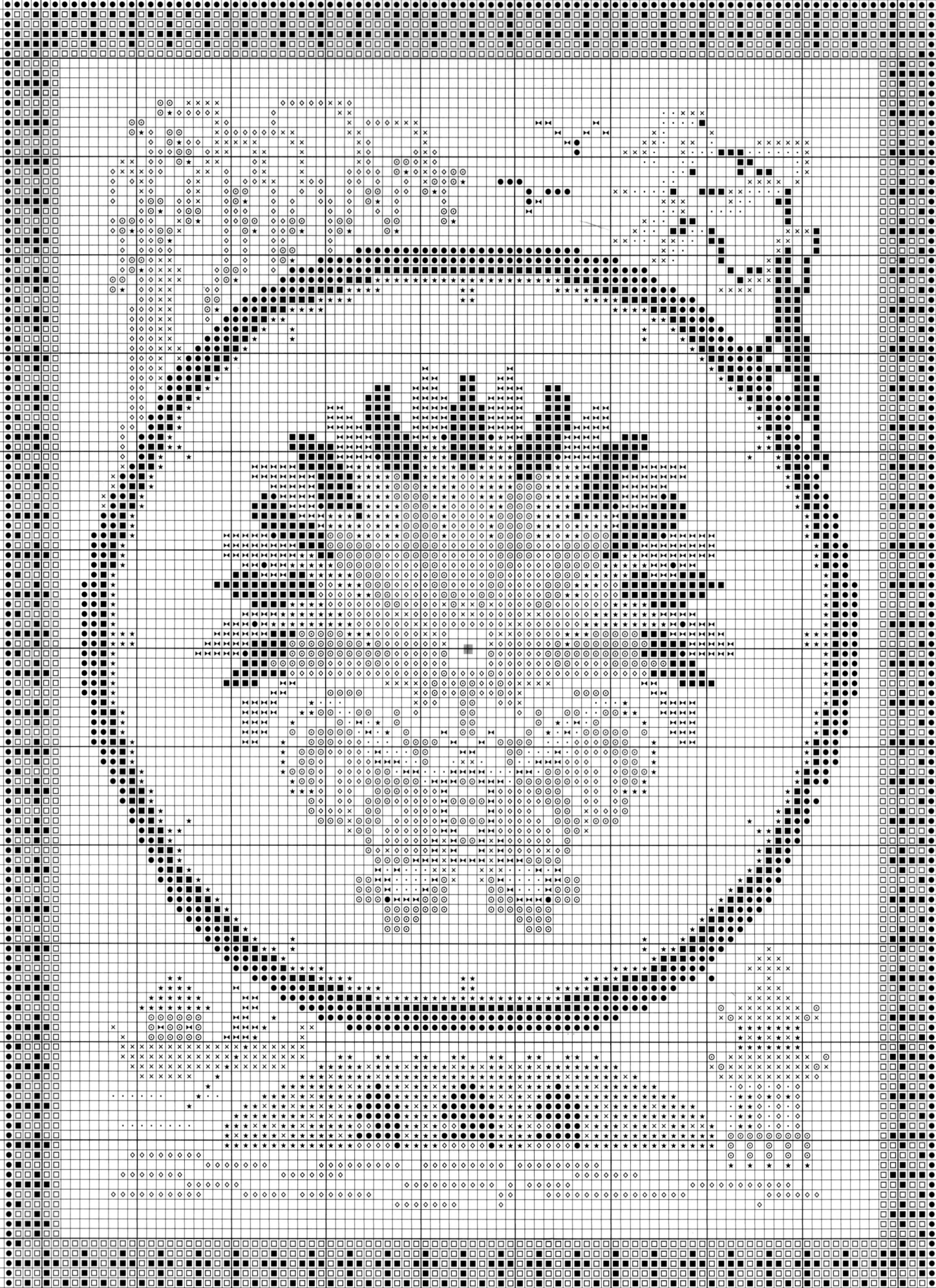

January

Designed by Elena Thomas

Time & Expertise

- Stitchers with a little experience will enjoy this project.
- This clock project can be completed in a month.

January Key

DMC		Colour
		Continental tent stitch in one strand
312	◇◇	Light blue
322	⊙⊙	Very light blue
336	××	Dark blue
517	··	Bright blue
743	□□	Yellow
796	■■	Medium blue
797	★★	Denim blue
823	●●	Light navy
939	▶◀	Dark navy

Fill in background with continental tent stitch in one strand of white

Our model was stitched using DMC Coton Perlé threads.

Finished size:
Stitch count 132 high x 98 wide

Fabric and approximate finished design area:
18HPI canvas 7⅜x5½in (19x14cm)

You Will Need

- 18HPI mono canvas – 11x9in (28x23cm), white
- DMC Coton Perlé – as listed in the key
- Tapestry needle – size 24
- Tapestry frame
- Clock – 7x9in (18x23cm) with 5x7in (4½x18cm) design area (Framecraft)
- Masking tape
- Needle – large-eyed for lacing
- Crochet cotton – for lacing

How to Stitch the Design

1. Do not use lengths of Coton Perlé any longer than 18in (45.5cm).

2. Use one strand to work the main blue and yellow pattern in continental tent stitch.

3. Start with a knot on the right side about 1½in (3.8cm) away from where you will begin stitching. Cut off the knot when the thread is securely stitched underneath.

4. Start stitching at the top of the canvas and gradually work downwards. This will prevent rubbing the work already stitched.

5. Stitch in a line or block completing one colour at a time. Take care not to jump over more than three holes to continue a colour, as this will create excess bulk on the wrong side.

6. Finish all the threads by working through a few stitches on the wrong side of the canvas. Do not leave any ends of threads dangling on the wrong side as these may become caught in the stitching.

7. When you have finished working the main pattern, fill in the background area – this is the blank space on the chart. Work with white Coton Perlé in continental tent stitch.

8. Refer to the guidelines page to see how to block and lace your stitched canvas.

9. Mount your stitching into the clock following the manufacturer's instructions.

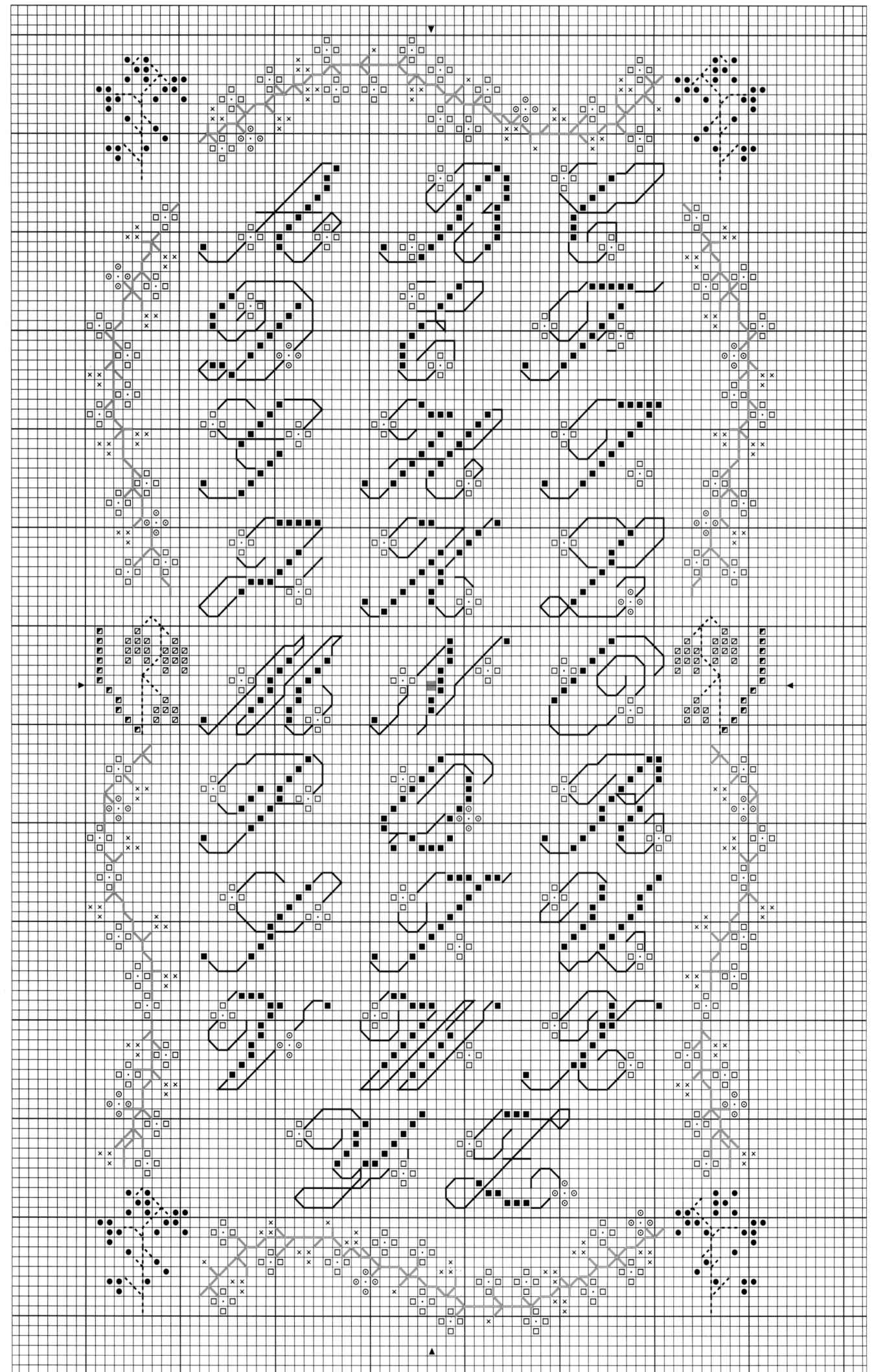

February

Designed by Rebecca Bradshaw

Time & Expertise

- The small scale of this project makes it suitable for an experienced stitcher.
- The sampler can be completed in about a month.

February Key

Madeira		Colour
Cross stitch in two strands		
0103	· ·	Yellow
0504	o o	Pink
0713	● ●	Mauve
106	▫ ▫	Light blue
107	⊠ ⊠	Dark blue
311	× ×	Light green
312	■ ■	Dark green
407	▨ ▨	Medium green
Backstitch in one strand		
311		Light green forget-me-not stems.
312		Dark green letters.
407		Medium green bluebell and violet stems.

Finished size:
Stitch count 132 high x 73 wide

Fabric and approximate finished Design area:
40HPI canvas 3⅜x1⅞in (7.8x4.8cm)

You Will Need

For the sampler:
- 40HPI silk gauze – 7½x6in (19x15.2cm), white
- Stranded cotton – as listed in the key
- Tapestry needle – size 26
- Mountboard – with 7x5½in (17.8x14cm) opening
- Masking tape
- Frame – 6x4½in (15.2x11.4cm), silver, decorative

For the monogram brooch
- 18HPI aida – 3x3in (7.6x7.6cm), white
- Stranded cotton – as for sampler
- Tapestry needle – size 26
- Brooch – 28mm round, silver finish (Elizabeth R Anderson)

How to Stitch the Design

1 Use masking tape to stick the edges of the silk gauze to the mount board. You will be using the mountboard frame as you would an embroidery hoop on other fabrics.

2 Work all the cross stitch in one strand of stranded cotton.

3 When you have finished all the cross stitch, work the backstitch detail in one strand: light green for the forget-me-not stems; dark green to outline the letters; medium green for the bluebell stems.

4 When you have completed your sampler, carefully remove it from the mount board then trim the gauze to fit your frame. We have attached our sampler to a piece of cream mount board to fit the inside of the frame.

March

Designed by Debra Page

You Will Need

For the sampler:
- **28HPI jobelan** – 15x12½in (38.1x31.8cm)
- **Stranded cotton** – as listed in the key
- **Tapestry needle** – size 26
- **Embroidery hoop** – or frame
- **Masking tape**
- **Frame** – 11¾x9½in (29.8x24.1cm), dark wood
- **Mount** – with an 8½x6¼in (21.6x15.9cm) opening
- **2oz wadding** – 8½x6¼in (21.6x15.9cm)

How to Stitch the Design

1. Work the whole design over two threads of the fabric.

2. The cross stitch is worked in two strands throughout. Work the half cross stitch also in two strands.

3. When you have completed all the cross stitch, work the backstitch in one strand of stranded cotton: dark pink to outline the butterflies and foxglove petals; dark blue to outline the bluebell petals; olive for the grass edges and primrose leaves; medium green for the outlines of the foxglove and bluebell leaves and stems; very dark brown to outline the treetrunks and branches, owl, deer, hedgehog, woodpecker, stoat, mushrooms and nest; black for the outlines of the squirrels, badger, blackbirds and mole; very dark green to outline the foliage and grass stumps.

4. Work the primroses in two strands of yellow in the star shape shown in the key.

5. Finally work the French knots in one strand: dark pink for the butterfly spots; light grey for the eyes of the woodpecker, badger, stoat and blackbirds; orange for the primrose centres; black for the squirrels' eyes, ends of butterfly antennae and the noses of the stoat and mole; very dark brown for the hedgehog's nose.

Time & Expertise

- Our woodland scene should take a month to complete.
- A stitcher with experience will enjoy this project.

March Key

Cross stitch in two strands

Anchor	DMC	Madeira	Colour
002	White	White	White
023	963	0608	Light pink
026	894	0414	Dark pink
047	321	0510	Red
131	798	0911	Light blue
233	451	1808	Dark grey
234	762	1709	Light grey
254	704	1308	V light green
255	907	1410	Light green
258	904	1413	Med green
268	937	1504	Dark green
291	444	0106	Yellow
359	898	2006	Dark brown
368	437	1910	Light brown
370	433	2303	Med brown
382	3371	2004	V dark brown
403	310	Black	Black
942	738	2013	Beige

Half cross stitch in two strands (bottom right to top left)

Anchor	DMC	Madeira	Colour
1216	094	1604/1606	Variegated greens

Cross stitch blending one strand of each

Anchor	DMC	Madeira	Colour
233	451	1808	Dark grey
234	762	1709	Light grey
368	437	1910	Light brown
370	433	2303	Med brown

Backstitch in one strand

Anchor	DMC	Madeira	Colour
026	894	0414	Dark pink outlines of butterflies and foxglove petals.
132	797	0912	Dark blue outlines of bluebell petals.
281	732	1613	Olive outlines of grass edges and primrose leaves.
258	904	1413	Medium green outlines of foxglove and bluebell leaves and stems.
382	3371	2004	Very dark brown outlines and details of tree trunks and branches, owl, deer, hedgehog, wood-pecker, stoat, mushrooms and nest.
403	310	Black	Black outlines of squirrels, badger, blackbirds and mole.
862	3362	1514	Very dark green outlines of foliage and grass stumps.

Long stitch in two strands

Anchor	DMC	Madeira	Colour
291	444	0106	Yellow primroses.

French knots in one strand

Anchor	DMC	Madeira	Colour
026	894	0414	Dark pink butterfly details.
234	762	1709	Light grey eyes.
314	741	0201	Orange centres of primroses.
382	3371	2004	Very dark brown hedgehog eye and nose and stoat nose.
403	310	Black	Black squirrel's eyes and ends of antennae, noses and of mole.

Finished size: Stitch count 120 high x 90 wide
Fabric and finished design area:
11HPI aida 11x8⅛in (28x20.8cm)
14HPI aida 8½x6½in (21.5x16.5cm)
18HPI aida 6⅝x5in (16.6x12.5cm)

April Key

Designed by Caroline Price

DMC	Anchor	Madeira		Colour
Cross stitch in two strands				
Ecru	387	Ecru		Ecru
310	403	Black		Black
437	362	2013		Light fawn
742	303	0114		Orange
3371	382	2004		V dark brown
Cross stitch blending one strand of each				
White 001	White	001		White
Ecru	387	Ecru		Ecru
Ecru	387	Ecru		Ecru
745	300	0111		Light cream
420	375	2105		Brown
437	362	2013		Light fawn
435	369	2010		Fawn
437	362	2013		Light fawn
676	891	2208		Light orange
745	300	0111		Light cream
Half cross stitch (bottom left to top right) in one strand				
524	858	1511		Light green
Half cross stitch (bottom left to top right) blending one strand of each				
518	168	1106		Aqua
524	858	1511		Light green
Glissengloss Sterling no.2				
522	860	1602		Dull green
524	858	1511		Light green
Half cross stitch (bottom right to top left) in one strand (see instructions)				
518	168	1106		Aqua
Half cross stitch in two strands (bottom left to top right)				
White 001	White			White
Backstitch in one strand				
310	403	Black		Black swan beak detail.
420	375	2105		Light brown background detail.
434	309	2009		Brown cygnet feathers (body).
610	889	2113		Taupe cygnet feathers (head).

Finished size:
Stitch count 72 high x 120 wide
Fabric and approximate design area:
11HPI aida 6⅝x11in (16.6x28cm)
14HPI aida 5¼x8⅝in (13.1x22.1cm)
18HPI aida 4x6¾in (10x16.9cm)

Time & Expertise

- This picture should take about a month to complete.
- An experienced stitcher will enjoy this project.

You Will Need

- **14HPI aida** – 13½x16¼in (34.3x41.3cm), pale grey
- **Stranded cotton** – as listed in the key
- **Tapestry needle** – size 24
- **Embroidery hoop** – or frame
- **Masking tape**
- **Frame** – 7½x10¼in (19x26cm), pale blue with gilt trim
- **2oz wadding** – 6x8¾in (15.2x22.2cm)

How to Stitch the Design

1 Work the cross stitch in two strands of stranded cotton. Some of the areas are stitched by combining one strand of two different colours in your needle to create a variegated effect. These areas are indicated in the key.

2 Work the half cross stitch (bottom left to top right) in the far background in one strand of light green. Blend one strand of light green and one strand of dull green for the greenery at the water's edge. The half cross stitches in the water are a blend of aqua, light green and Glissengloss.

3 To create the shadow under the swan and cygnets, shown by the symbol 'x', work the first half of the stitch (bottom left to top right) using one strand of aqua, light green and Glissengloss. To complete the cross stitch (bottom right to top left), work with one strand of aqua.

4 When you have finished all the cross stitch and half stitches, work the backstitch in one strand of stranded cotton: black for the swan's beak detail; light brown for the background detail; brown for the feathers on the cygnet's body; taupe for the feathers on the cygnet's head. Use two strands of white for the swan's eye detail.

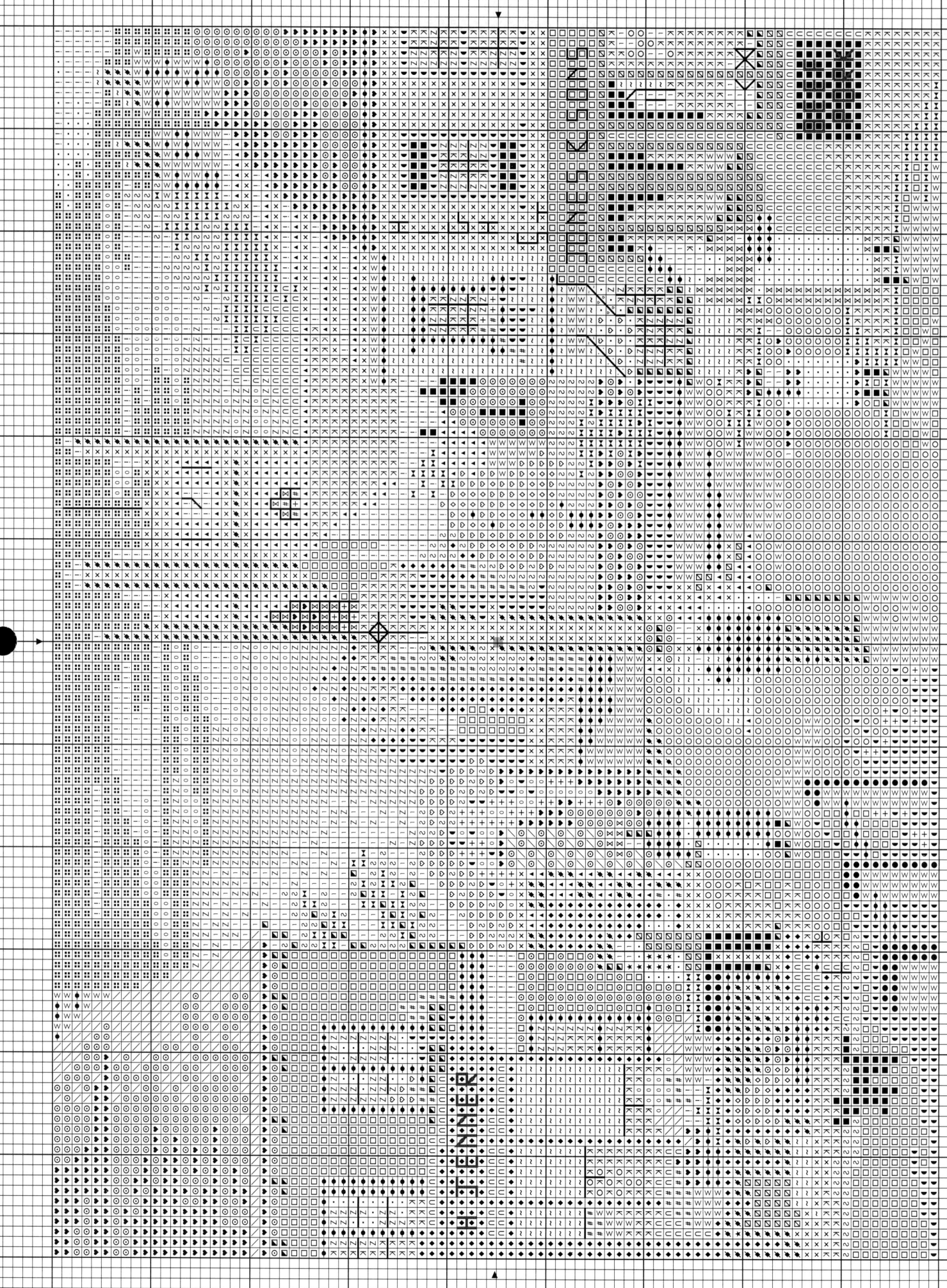

Designed by Lesley Grant

Time & Expertise

- Our village scene will take around six weeks to complete.
- This project is suitable for a stitcher with a little experience.

You Will Need

- **12HPI mono interlock canvas** – 16½x19in (42x48cm), white
- **DMC Tapestry wool:**
  1 skein: 7133, 7170, 7174, 7176, 7270, 7273, 7275, 7302, 7320, 7322, 7323, 7376, 7402, 7406, 7450, 7468, 7469, 7497, 7503, 7506, 7523, 7604, 7713, 7727, 7905, 7917, 7949, 7988, White
  2 skeins: 7452, 7715, 7950
- **DMC Stranded cotton** – 844, White
- **Tapestry needles** – size 18, size 24
- **Tapestry frame**
- **Frame** – 13½x15in (34.5x38cm), green with gilt trim
- **Mount** – with a 7½x10in (19x25.5cm) opening, light green
- **2oz wadding** – 7½x10in (19x25.5cm)
- **Scissors**
- **Masking tape**
- **Mounting board** – to fit inside your frame, for lacing on to
- **Needle** – large-eyed for lacing
- **Crochet cotton** – for lacing

How to Stitch the Design

1. Do not use lengths of wool any longer than 18in (45.5cm).

2. Use one strand of wool and work in continental tent stitch for the main stitching.

3. Start with a knot on the right side about 1½in (3.8cm) away from where you will begin stitching. Cut off the knot when the thread is securely stitched underneath.

4. Start stitching at the top of the canvas and gradually work downwards. This will prevent rubbing of the work already stitched.

5. Stitch in a line or block completing one colour at a time. Take care not to jump over more than three holes of the canvas to continue a colour, as this will create excess bulk on the wrong side.

6. Finish all your threads by working through a few stitches on the wrong side. Do not leave any ends of threads dangling on the wrong side as these may become accidentally caught in the stitching.

7. When you have finished working all the continental tent stitches, work the backstitch detail in three strands of stranded cotton; white for the lettering on the blackboard and greengrocer's stand and dark grey for the lettering on the butcher's shop, window details, flagpole, clock face and spire.

May Key

DMC	Anchor	Appletons	Symbol	Colour
\multicolumn{5}{l}{Continental tent stitch in one strand of tapestry wool}
White	8002	991	· ·	White
7133	8342	942	♡♡	Pink
7170	8542	877	1 1	Light pink
7174	9510	123	⊙⊙	Light tan
7176	9562	479	♥♥	Tan
7270	9772	961	× ×	Light grey
7273	9774	963	▲▲	Grey
7275	9794	965	✱✱	Dark grey
7302	8686	462	⊠⊠	Blue
7320	9204	404	◆◆	Green
7322	8872	521	Z Z	Light turquoise
7323	8894	152	⁝⁝	Turquoise
7376	9264	357	◀◀	Dull green
7402	9014	401	s s	Light mint green
7406	9078	294	⋈⋈	Mint green
7450	9632	988	ǀ ǀ	Ecru
7452	8296	705	□□	Beige
7468	9648	585	●●	Dark brown
7469	9666	589	▨▨	Very dark brown
7497	9496	305	◆◆	Brown
7503	8054	851	~ ~	Light gold
7506	8140	475	⊠⊠	Gold
7523	9384	951	n n	Very light green

DMC	Anchor	Appletons	Symbol	Colour
7604	8982	431	◇◇	Bright green
7713	9798	998	■■	Dk charcoal grey
7715	8624	741	✕✕	Charcoal grey
7727	8114	552	++	Yellow
7905	8032	871	o o	Light yellow
7917	8324	861	◣◣	Light orange
7949	8506	931	≶≶	Dark flesh
7950	9508	203	◯◯	Light flesh
7988	9204	545	# #	Grass green

DMC	Anchor	Madeira	Symbol	Description
\multicolumn{5}{l}{Backstitch in three strands of embroidery cotton}
White	White	001		White lettering on blackboard and greengrocer's sign.
844	401	1809		Dark grey lettering on butcher's shop window details, flagpole, clock face

Finished size: Stitch count 90 high x 120 wide
Fabric and approximate finished design

Time & Expertise

- Our wedding sampler can be completed in about three weeks.
- With care, a beginner will be able to attempt this project.

Designed by Alison Burton

You Will Need

- **28HPI evenweave** – 16x14in (40.6x35.6cm), magnolia
- **Stranded cotton** – as listed in the key
- **Tapestry needle** – size 26
- **Embroidery hoop** – or frame
- **Masking tape**
- **Frame** – 12x10in (30.5x25.4cm), peach
- **2oz wadding** – 10½x8½in (26.7x21.6cm)

How to Stitch the Design

1. Work the whole design over two threads of the fabric.

2. Work the border roses and their leaves in one strand of stranded cotton. The rest of the cross stitch is worked in two strands.

3. When you have completed all the cross stitch, backstitch all the lettering in two strands of dark peach. The full alphabet is charted for you to add the names and date of your choice.

4. Work the rest of the backstitch using one strand of stranded cotton: dark peach to outline the inner borders; very dark grey for the outlines and details on the groom and arch; dark grey for the outlines and details on the bride; green for the rose stalks.

5. Finally, work the French knots in one strand: dark peach for the brides head-dress and the dots on the letter i (where appropriate); light peach for the bride's headdress; very dark grey for the groom's eyes; dark grey for the bride's eyes and the buttons on her dress.

June Key

DMC	Anchor	Madeira		Colour
Cross stitch in one strand				
353	008	0304		Light peach
502	216	1513		Green
Cross stitch in two strands				
White	002	White		White
352	010	0406		Dark peach
353	008	0304		Light peach
413	401	1713		Very dark grey
414	235	1801		Dark grey
415	398	1803		Light grey
451	233	1808		Medium grey
502	216	1513		Green
840	354	1912		Brown
948	778	0306		Flesh
Backstitch in one strand				
352	010	0406		Dark peach outlines of inner borders.
413	401	1713		Very dark grey outlines and details on groom and arch.
414	235	1801		Dark grey outlines and details of bride's dress and face.
502	216	1513		Green rose stalks.
840	354	1912		Brown bride's hair detail.
Backstitch in two strands				
352	010	0406		Dark peach lettering.
French knots in one strand				
352	010	0406		Dark peach brides head dress & dots on letter 'i's.
353	008	0304		Light peach bride's headdress.
413	401	1713		Very dark grey groom's eyes.
414	235	1801		Dark grey bride's eyes and buttons on dress.

Finished size: Stitch count 120 high x 90 wide
Fabric and finished design area:
11HPI aida 11x8⅛in (28x21.1cm)
28HPI evenweave 8½x6½in (21.5x16.5cm)
18HPI aida 6⅝x5in (16.6x12.5cm)

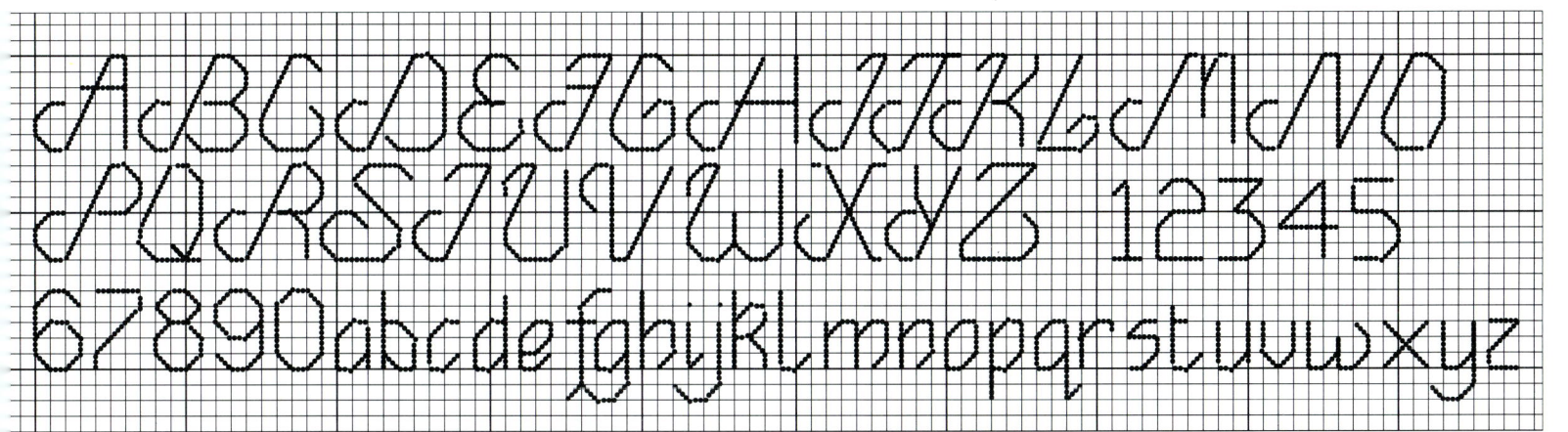

January

Sunday	Monday	Tuesday	Wednesday	Thursday	Friday	Saturday
1 *New Moon, New Year's Day*	2 *Bank Holiday, UK & Eire*	3	4	5	6	7
8	9	10	11	12	13	14
15	16 *Full Moon*	17	18	19	20	21
22	23	24	25	26	27	28
29	30 *New Moon*	31			*December* S M T W T F S 1 2 3 4 5 6 7 8 9 10 11 12 13 14 15 16 17 18 19 20 21 22 23 24 25 26 27 28 29 30 31	*February* S M T W T F S 1 2 3 4 5 6 7 8 9 10 11 12 13 14 15 16 17 18 19 20 21 22 23 24 25 26 27 28

February

Sunday	Monday	Tuesday	Wednesday	Thursday	Friday	Saturday
	January S M T W T F S 1 2 3 4 5 6 7 8 9 10 11 12 13 14 15 16 17 18 19 20 21 22 23 24 25 26 27 28 29 30 31		1	2	3	4
5	6	7	8	9	10	11
12	13	14 Valentine's Day	15 Full Moon	16	17	18
19	20	21	22	23	24	25
26	27	28 Shrove Tuesday				

March S M T W T F S 1 2 3 4 5 6 7 8 9 10 11 12 13 14 15 16 17 18 19 20 21 22 23 24 25 26 27 28 29 30 31

March

February
S M T W T F S
     1 2 3 4
5 6 7 8 9 10 11
12 13 14 15 16 17 18
19 20 21 22 23 24 25
26 27 28

April
S M T W T F S
30   1
2 3 4 5 6 7 8
9 10 11 12 13 14 15
16 17 18 19 20 21 22
23 24 25 26 27 28 29

Sunday	Monday	Tuesday	Wednesday	Thursday	Friday	Saturday
			1 Ash Wednesday / St David's Day / New Moon	2	3	4
5	6	7	8	9	10	11
12	13	14	15	16	17 St Patrick's Day / Full Moon	18
19	20	21	22	23	24	25
26 Summer Time Begins / Mothering Sunday	27	28	29	30	31 New Moon	

May

Sunday	Monday	Tuesday	Wednesday	Thursday	Friday	Saturday
	1 *Bank Holiday Scotland, Eire*	2	3	4	5	6
7	8 *May Day Bank Holiday England, NI, Scotland, Eire*	9	10	11	12	13
14 *Full Moon*	15	16	17	18	19	20
21	22	23	24	25	26	27
28	29 *New Moon* *Bank Holiday NI,* *England, Scotland,* *Wales, Eire*	30	31			

April
S	M	T	W	T	F	S
30						1
2	3	4	5	6	7	8
9	10	11	12	13	14	15
16	17	18	19	20	21	22
23	24	25	26	27	28	29

June
S	M	T	W	T	F	S
				1	2	3
4	5	6	7	8	9	10
11	12	13	14	15	16	17
18	19	20	21	22	23	24
25	26	27	28	29	30	

June

| | *May*
S M T W T F S
1 2 3 4 5 6
7 8 9 10 11 12 13
14 15 16 17 18 19 20
21 22 23 24 25 26 27
28 29 30 31 | *July*
S M T W T F S
                              1
2 3 4 5 6 7 8
9 10 11 12 13 14 15
16 17 18 19 20 21 22
23 24 25 26 27 28 29
30 31 |

Sunday	Monday	Tuesday	Wednesday	Thursday	Friday	Saturday
				1	2	3
4	5 *Bank Holiday Eire*	6	7	8	9	10
11	12	13 *Full Moon*	14	15	16	17
18 *Father's Day*	19	20	21 *Longest Day*	22	23	24
25	26	27	28 *New Moon*	29	30	

November

Sunday	Monday	Tuesday	Wednesday	Thursday	Friday	Saturday
October S M T W T F S 1 2 3 4 5 6 7 8 9 10 11 12 13 14 15 16 17 18 19 20 21 22 23 24 25 26 27 28 29 30 31	*December* S M T W T F S 1 2 3 4 5 6 7 8 9 10 11 12 13 14 15 16 17 18 19 20 21 22 23 24 25 26 27 28 29 30 31		1	2	3	4
5 *Bonfire Night*	6	7 *Full Moon*	8	9	10	11
12 *Rememberence Sunday*	13	14	15	16	17	18
19	20	21	22 *New Moon*	23	24	25
26	27	28	29	30 *St Andrew's Day*		

December

November
S M T W T F S
　 　 1 2 3 4
5 6 7 8 9 10 11
12 13 14 15 16 17 18
19 20 21 22 23 24 25
26 27 28 29 30

January
S M T W T F S
　 1 2 3 4 5 6
7 8 9 10 11 12 13
14 15 16 17 18 19 20
21 22 23 24 25 26 27
28 29 30 31

Sunday	Monday	Tuesday	Wednesday	Thursday	Friday	Saturday
					1	2
3	4	5	6	7 Full Moon	8	9
10	11	12	13	14	15	16
17	18	19	20	21 Shortest Day	22 New Moon	23
24 / 31	25 Christmas Day	26 Boxing Day	27	28	29	30

Time & Expertise

- You can complete this design in a couple of weeks.
- With care, a beginner can stitch this cross stitch picture.

Designed by Evelyn King

You Will Need

- **28HPI evenweave** – 16¼x14in (41x35.5cm), cream
- **Stranded cotton** – as listed in the key
- **Tapestry needle** – size 26
- **Frame** – 12¼x10in (31x25.5cm), green wood with gilt trim
- **Mounts** – two, with a 8¼x6in (21x15cm) oval inner opening, one pink, one green
- **2oz wadding** – 8¼x6in (21x15cm), oval shape

How to Stitch the Design

1. Work the whole design over two threads of the fabric.
2. The cross stitch is worked in one strand throughout.
3. When you have completed all the cross stitch, work the backstitch in one strand of stranded cotton: dark grey for the ironwork and details on the well base; medium grey for the detail at the far end of the path and on the well base; dark pink for the rose outlines; cream for the top right and right side outline of the well base; dark brown for the trellis details; khaki for the rose stems and the greenery detail.

July Key

DMC	Anchor	Madeira		Colour
Cross stitch in one strand				
413	401	1713		Dark grey
414	235	1801		Medium grey
415	398	1803		Light grey
451	233	1808		Dark pink/grey
452	232	1807		Medium pink/grey
453	397	1806		Light pink/grey
471	266	1408		Light green
603	051	0614		Dark pink
605	050	0613		Medium pink
738	361	2013		Beige
745	300	0111		Yellow
746	386	0101		Cream
841	378	1911		Light brown
844	401	1809		Very dark grey
890	218	1314		Dark green
937	268	1504		Khaki
988	243	1402		Medium green
3032	392	1903		Medium brown
3689	049	0607		Light pink

DMC	Anchor	Madeira		Colour
Backstitch in one strand				
413	401	1713		Dark grey iron work and details on well base.
414	235	1801		Medium grey detail at end of perspective and details on well base.
603	051	0614		Dark pink rose outlines.
746	386	0101		Cream details on well base.
840	354	1912		Dark brown trellis details.
937	268	1504		Khaki stems and greenery.

Our model was stitched using DMC threads; the Anchor and Madeira conversions are not necessarily exact colour equivalents.

Finished size:
Stitch count 106 high x 62 wide

Fabric and finished design area:
11HPI aida 9⅝x5⅝in (25x14cm)
28HPI aida 7½x4½in (19x11.5cm)
18HPI aida 5⅞x3½in (15x9cm)

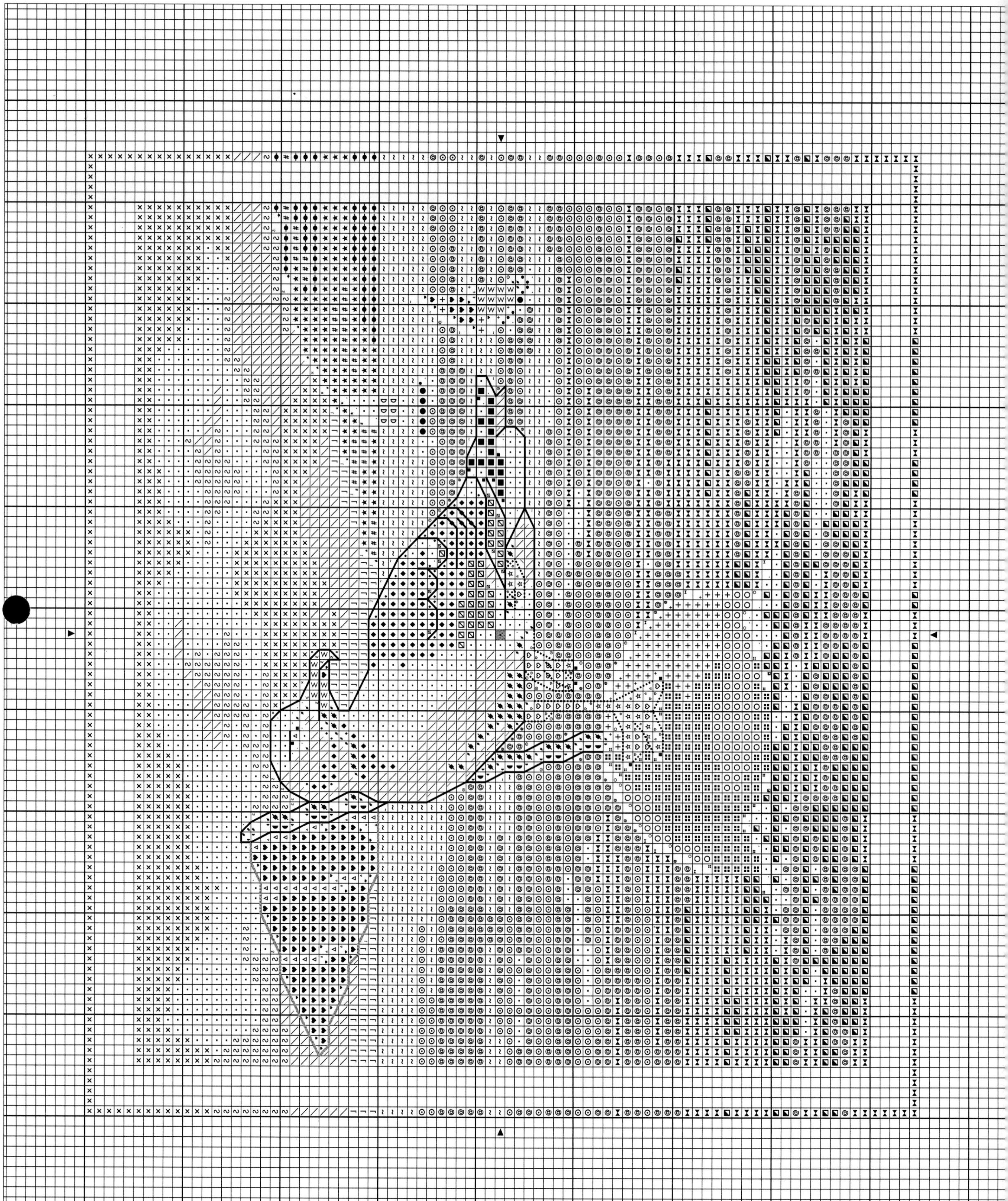

August

Designed by Alison Burton

Time & Expertise

- You can complete this design in a less than a month.
- We recommend this project for experienced stitchers.

You Will Need

- 14HPI aida – 13x14in (33x35.5cm), white
- Stranded cotton – as listed in the key
- Tapestry needle – size 24
- Embroidery hoop – or frame
- Masking tape
- Frame – 10x11in (25.5x28cm), blue wood with gilt trim
- 2oz wadding – 8x9in (20x23cm)

How to Stitch the Design

1. Bind the edges of the aida with masking tape or machine zig-zag around it to prevent the fabric from fraying.

2. Mount your fabric in an embroidery hoop or frame to help keep the tension of your stitches even.

3. Work the cross stitch in two strands of stranded cotton. Some of the areas are stitched by blending one strand of two different colours in your needle. This creates a variegated effect. These areas are indicated in the key.

4. Some areas (around the buoy, on the gull, on the flag and flagpole, where the land meets the sky) are worked using quarter and three-quarter stitches. These are shown on the chart and also explained in the guidelines pages.

5. When you have finished all the cross stitch, work the backstitch detail in one strand of stranded cotton: dark grey for the gull and flag pole outlines and detail; red for the outline of the flag; dark brown for the outlines of the gull's legs.

August Key

DMC	Anchor	Madeira		Colour
Cross stitch in two strands				
White	002	White		White
307	289	0104		Light yellow
310	403	Black		Black
317	400	1714		Dark grey
318	399	1801		Light grey
402	313	2301		Light terracotta
444	291	0106		Dark yellow
666	046	0210		Red
726	295	0109		Medium yellow
762	397	1804		Very light grey
924	851	1706		Dark turquoise
926	850	1707		Med turquoise
927	849	1708		Light turquoise
930	922	1712		Dark blue
3325	128	1013		Medium blue
3752	343	1710		Light blue
3753	158	1001		Very light blue
3768	840	1704		Blue/grey
3776	326	0310		Med terracotta
3781	905	2106		Dark brown

DMC	Anchor	Madeira		Colour
Cross stitch blending one strand of each				
318	399	1801		Light grey
932	920	0710		Light denim
318	399	1801		Light grey
3753	158	1001		Very light blue
355	340	0401		Dark terracotta
666	046	0210		Red
444	291	0106		Dark yellow
3045	374	2104		Light brown
501	878	1705		Green/blue
926	850	1707		Med turquoise

DMC	Anchor	Madeira		Colour
762	397	1804		Very light grey
3752	343	1710		Light blue
926	850	1707		Med turquoise
3790	904	1905		Dull brown
927	849	1708		Light turquoise
3768	840	1704		Blue/grey
Backstitch in one strand				
317	400	1714		Dark grey gull and flag pole outlines and details.
666	046	0210		Red flag outlines.
3781	905	2106		Dark brown gull's legs and wing detail.

Our model was stitched using DMC threads; the Anchor and Madeira conversions are not necessarily exact colour equivalents.

Finished size:
Stitch count 95 high x 85 wide

Fabric and approximate finished design area:
11HPI aida 8⅝x7¾in (22x19.75cm)
14HPI aida 6¾x6in (17x15cm)
18HPI aida 5¼x4¾in (13.5x12cm)

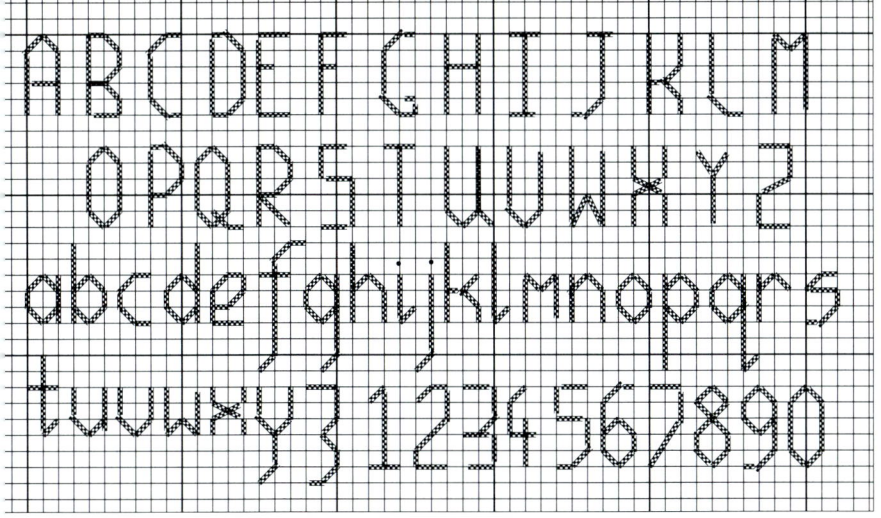

Time & Expertise

- You can complete this design in under a month.
- Stitchers with some experience will enjoy stitching this cross stitch picture.

You Will Need

- 14HPI aida – 16¼x14¼in (42x36cm), cream
- Stranded cotton – as listed in the key
- Tapestry needle – size 24
- Embroidery hoop – or frame
- Masking tape
- Frame – 11¼x9¼in (28.5x23.5cm), red
- 2oz wadding – 9½x7½in (25x19cm)

Designed by Lynda Whittle

How to Stitch the Design

1 Work all the cross stitch first in two strands of stranded cotton.

2 Work the following backstitch details in one strand: red for the outlines of the hearts and the bear's bow tie; grey for the outlines of the toys, the letters on the toys and balloons and the kite bow details; dark brown for the outline and details on the arms, legs and head of bear; black for the outlines of the bear's pupils, waistcoat and the clowns eye; purple for the outline of the flower.

3 The balloons are outlined in one strand using the same colour; blue for the blue balloon, red for the red balloon and so on. Backstitch the outlines of the kites using one strand of the darker shade; dark purple for no.1 kite, dark green for no.2 kite and so on.

4 Use two strands of black to backstitch the kite and balloon strings and three strands to work the numbers on the brightly coloured kites.

5 Work the French knots in three strands: white for the bear's eyes; black for the clown's eyes.

6 Finally, use two strands of dark green to backstitch the name and birth details of your choice. Use two strands of dark green for the French knots on the dots of the 'i's in the lettering.

September Key

Anchor DMC Madeira   Colour
Cross stitch in two strands

Anchor	DMC	Madeira		Colour
001	White	White	··	White
046	666	0210	++	Red
050	605	0613	⋈⋈	Pink
087	3607	0709	∷∷	Dark mauve
096	3609	0710	--	Light mauve
101	552	0713	☆☆	Purple
130	799	1004	××	Light blue
133	796	0913	⌀⌀	Dark blue
185	964	1112	●●	Turquoise
227	701	1305	■■	Medium green
241	955	1211	○○	Light green
246	319	1405	₂₂	Dark green
291	444	0106	∘∘	Yellow
330	947	0205	▲▲	Orange
369	435	2010	//	Light brown
403	310	Black	●●	Black
410	995	1102	▲▲	Bright blue

Backstitch in one strand

046	666	0210		Red outlines of hearts and details and outline of bear's bow tie.
236	413	1713		Grey outlines of toys, letters on toys, balloons, details on kite bows.
360	898	2006		Dark brown bear main outlines.
403	310	Black		Black bear's pupils and waistcoat details and clown's eye.
				Self colour outlines of kites, bows purple petals and centre, use colour as for cross stitched area – for kites use the darker colour.

Anchor	DMC	Madeira		Colour
Backstitch in two strands				
403	310	Black		Black kite and balloon strings
246	319	1405		Dark green lettering.
Backstitch in three strands				
403	310	Black		Black numbers on kites.
French knots in three strands				
001	White	White		White teddy's eyes.
403	310	Black		Black clown's eyes.
French knots in two strands				
246	319	1405		Dark green dots on the letters.

Our model was stitched using Anchor threads; the DMC and Madeira conversions are not necessarily exact colour equivalents.

Finished size:
Stitch count 120 high x 90 wide

Fabric and approximate finished design area:
11HPI aida 11x8⅛in (28x21cm)
14HPI aida 8½x6½in (21x16.5cm)
18HPI aida 6⅝x5in (17x13cm)

October

Designed by Jane Randall

How to Stitch the Design

1. Bind the edges of the evenweave with masking tape or machine zig-zag around it to prevent the fabric from fraying.

2. Mount your fabric in an embroidery hoop or frame to help keep the tension of your stitches even.

3. Work the cross stitch first in two strands of stranded cotton.

4. When you have finished all the cross stitch, work the backstitch detail in one strand of stranded cotton: dark green for the crocodiles' outlines and details; dark brown for the outlines and details of the snails, coloured birds, squirrels, ostriches' heads and necks, camels, ark and animals on the ark (except the elephant); dark grey for the outlines and details of the seals, rhinos, dove, unicorns, ostriches' bodies, sheep, penguins fronts and rabbits; black to outline the backs of the two penguins.

5. Finally, work the French knots in one strand of stranded cotton: dark green for the crocodiles' eyes; dark brown for the snails' antennae, eyes of the squirrels, ostriches, camel, animals on ark (except the elephant) and coloured birds; dark grey for the eyes of the seals, rhinos, doves, unicorns, sheep, rabbits and elephant. The penguins' eyes are worked by stitching a dark grey French knot over a loose, white French knot.

Time & Expertise

- You can complete this design in under a month.
- A stitcher with some experience will enjoy this cross stitch project.

You Will Need

- 28HPI evenweave – 15x13¾in (38x35cm), cream
- Stranded cotton – as listed in the key
- Tapestry needle – size 26
- Embroidery hoop – or frame
- Masking tape
- Frame – 12x10¾in (30.5x27cm),
- Mount – with a 7⅞x6½in (20x16.5cm) opening, creamy yellow
- 2oz wadding – 7⅞x6½in (20x16.5cm)

October Key

Anchor	DMC	Madeira	Colour
Cross stitch in two strands			
White	002	White	White
160	813	1012	Blue
241	955	1213	Light green
245	986	1405	Dark green
305	743	0110	Yellow
308	782	2212	Medium brown
314	741	0201	Orange
366	951	1909	Light brown
371	433	2008	Dark brown
398	415	1803	Light grey
400	317	1714	Dark grey
403	310	Black	Black

Anchor	DMC	Madeira	Colour
Backstitch in one strand			
245	986	1405	Dark green outlines and details of crocodiles.
310	403	Black	Black penguin details.
371	433	2008	Dark brown outlines and details of snails, coloured birds, squirrels, ostriches' heads and necks, camels, ark and animals on ark (except elephant) kangaroos, snakes, tortoises.
400	317	1714	Dark grey outlines and details of seals, rhinos, dove, unicorns, ostriches bodies, sheep, penguins, elephants zebras and rabbits.

Anchor	DMC	Madeira	Colour
French knots in one strand			
245	986	1405	Dark green crocodiles eyes.
371	433	2008	Dark brown antennae ends of snails, eyes of squirrels, ostriches' heads and necks, camels, ark and animals on ark (except elephant), coloured birds.
400	317	1714	Dark grey eyes of seals, rhinos, dove, unicorns, ostriches bodies, sheep, penguins and rabbits.

French knots in one strand grey on top of white

Anchor	DMC	Madeira	Colour
002	White	White	White
400	317	1714	Dark grey penguin eyes.

Our model was stitched using Anchor threads; the DMC and Madeira conversions are not necessarily exact colour equivalents.

Finished size:
Stitch count 112 high x 90 wide

Fabric and finished design area:
11HPI aida 10⅛x8⅛in (24x20cm)
28HPI evenweave 8x6½in (20x16.5cm)
18HPI aida 6¼x5in (16x13cm)

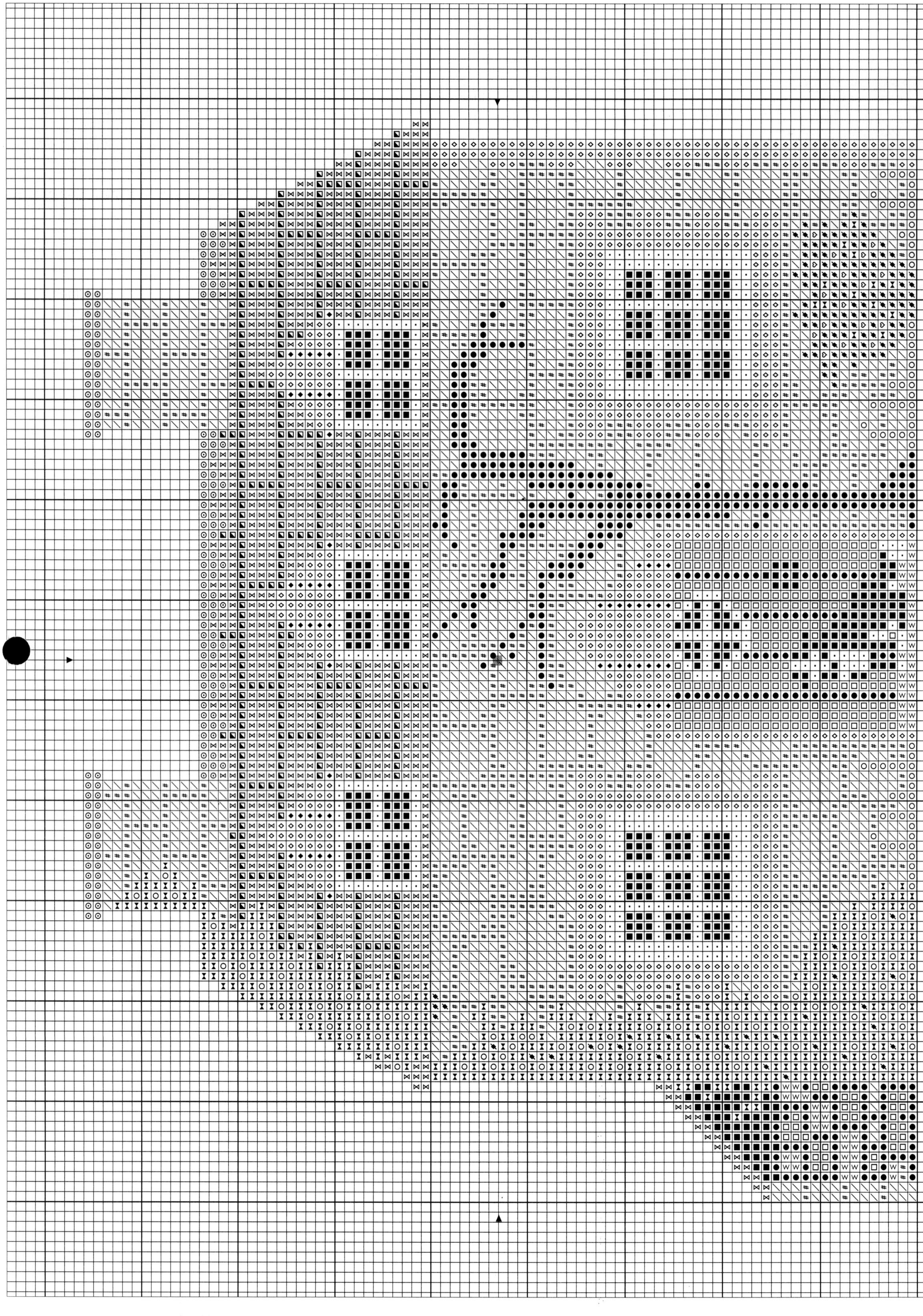

Time & Expertise

- You can complete this design in a less than a month.
- We recommend this project for experienced stitchers.

Designed by Debra Cowell

You Will Need

- 10HPI mono interlock canvas – 12½x15in (31.5x38cm), antique
- DMC needlepoint wool:
  1 skein: 7303, 7345, 7347, 7348, 7544, 7622, 7695, 7739, 7846, 7938, Black 2 skeins: 7273, 7304, 7503, 7511, White
- Tapestry needle – size 16
- Masking tape
- Tapestry frame
- Backing fabric – cotton, 12x45in (30.5x114cm)
- Plain lining fabric – cotton, 12x45in (30.5x114cm) for lining
- 4oz wadding – 10x24in (25.5x61cm)
- Matching thread
- Usual sewing kit – including needle, pins, scissors etc.

November Key

DMC	Anchor	Appletons		Colour
Blanc	8000	991B	∙∙	White
7273	9676	964	✗✗	Med grey
7303	8312	726	○○	Terracotta
7304	8820	462	◇◇	Light blue
7345	9120	428	○○	Light green
7347	9028	407	✹✹	Dark green
7348	8992	405	⋈⋈	Med green
7503	8054	691	∕∕	Light cream
7511	9674	981	##	Light grey
7544	8218	448	♡♡	Red
7622	9764	966	◤◤	Dark grey
7695	8824	747	◆◆	Dark blue
7739	8058	693	≤≤	Dark cream
7846	8102	695	□□	Tan
7938	9644	187	●●	Brown
Noir	9800	993	■■	Black

Tent stitch in one strand

Finished size:
Stitch count 86 high x 108 wide
Fabric and approximate finished design area:
10HPI canvas 8⅝x10⅞in (23x28cm)

How to Stitch the Design

1. Fold the canvas lightly in half both ways to find the centre and mark this with a pin. This is the best place to begin stitching and is indicated on the chart by a grey square.

2. Bind the raw edges of the canvas with masking tape. This will prevent them from unravelling or snagging the wool.

3. Attach the canvas to a frame. This will help to stop it distorting.

4. Cut the wool into 20in (51cm) lengths. If the wool is much longer it will stretch and tangle.

5. Work the design using one strand of tapestry wool.

6. Start with a knot on the right side of the canvas about 1½in (3.8cm) away from your first stitch. Cut off the knot when the thread has been secured with the first few stitches.

7. Finish the thread by working through a few stitches on the wrong side.

8. Work the design in continental tent stitch.

How to Block your Canvas
You Will Need

- Flat clean board
- Blotting paper
- Drawing pins

1. If the canvas has very little distortion after stitching, it will only need to be lightly steam pressed to even out the stitched surface. Place your finished work face down on a clean cloth, place another cloth on top and press until dry.

2. If your canvas is not square, then lightly dampen or spray it with water to soften it a bit. Now mark the finished size of the canvas on to the blotting paper and place the canvas face down on it.

3. Place the canvas squarely to match up with the drawn lines on the paper. Pin the canvas, outside the stitched area, on to the board. When it is completely dry, it can be made up. The drying process may take several days.

How to Make the Cosy

1. Cut the canvas to ½in (13mm) outside the stitching area all the way around. Pin the canvas and the backing fabric wrong sides together and cut out the fabric to the same shape as the canvas.

2. Place the stitched canvas on to the lining fabric wrong sides together and cut out the fabric to the same shape. Repeat this with the backing fabric, wrong sides together.

3. Place the stitched canvas over the wadding and cut around the shape. Turn the canvas over and cut another piece of wadding to this shape.

4. Place one lining piece right side down with a piece of wadding over it then the stitched canvas right side up over that. Tack together around all the edges. Repeat this with the other piece of lining, wadding and backing fabric.

5. Cut two binding strips 2x12in (5x30.5cm) for the top and bottom of the cosy and one strip 2x35in (5x89cm) for the edges.

6. Take one of the shorter binding strips and pin it right sides together to the lower edge of the front of the cosy. Stitch it in place by hand or machine ½in (13mm) from the edge. If you are stitching by hand, use backstitch. Turn the strip over to the cosy lining. Fold under the raw edge of the strip and slip stitch to the lining. Repeat this process for the back of the cosy with the other shorter binding strip.

7. With lining sides together pin then tack the front of the cosy to the back around the shaped edge. Turn under one end of the remaining strip ½in (13mm), then pin it to the front of the cosy right side down all around the curved edge. The strip should line up with the edge of the cosy and enclose the strips on the bottom of the front and back. Trim then turn under ½in (13mm) at the other end of the strip so that it fits exactly round the cosy.

8. Stitch ½in (13mm) in from the edge, gently easing the strip around the curves and taking care not to stretch the strip too much. You should secure the turned ends of the strip with stitches for a neat finish.

9. Turn the strip over to the back of the teacosy. Fold under the raw edge and slip stitch it into place.